Exploring Infrastructure

AIRPORTS

Jeff Mapua

Enslow Publishing
101 W. 23rd Street
Suite 240
New York, NY 10011
USA

enslow.com

Published in 2020 by Enslow Publishing, LLC.
101 W. 23rd Street, Suite 240, New York, NY 10011

Library of Congress Cataloging-in-Publication Data

Names: Mapua, Jeff, author.
Title: Airports / Jeff Mapua.
Description: New York : Enslow Publishing, [2020] | Series: Exploring infrastructure | Audience: Grade 3-6. | Includes bibliographical references and index.
Identifiers: LCCN 2018004902| ISBN 9781978503328 (library bound) | ISBN 9781978505063 (pbk.)
Subjects: LCSH: Airports—Juvenile literature. | Air travel—Juvenile literature. | Architecture, Modern—21st century.
Classification: LCC TL725.15 .M37 2018 | DDC 387.7/36—dc23
LC record available at https://lccn.loc.gov/2018004902

Printed in the United States of America

To Our Readers: We have done our best to make sure all website addresses in this book were active and appropriate when we went to press. However, the author and the publisher have no control over and assume no liability for the material available on those websites or on any websites they may link to. Any comments or suggestions can be sent by email to customerservice@enslow.com.

CONTENTS

1017

INTRODUCTION

Meet Clare Beadle. She has a very interesting job. One day, she got a call that a large spider had escaped its cage on an airplane. The spider was walking down the aisle of the plane! Clare does not like spiders herself, but it was her job to find it. "I don't like eight-legged creatures," she said. Clare knew she had to find the spider. Then she would have to capture and rescue it.

Clare works at Gatwick Airport. It is one of the busiest airports in London, England. Clare is a manager of the Animal Reception Centre. Her job is to take care of the airport's nonhuman passengers. She prepares animals for flights, checks them in, and makes sure they have the proper paperwork. Clare and her coworkers let people (like the plane's captain) know about the animals. She also makes sure that there is someone to pick them up when the plane lands.

Ready for Takeoff

When an animal is ready for flight, it is placed on the plane. Many people think that animals are stored along with luggage. That is

Gatwick Airport in London, England

not true. They are placed safely in a part of the plane that has the proper temperature.

Clare carefully makes sure that each animal is put on the correct plane. In ten years, she has never sent an animal to the wrong place. Clare and her coworkers treat each animal like their own. They have had a wide variety of animals to take care of, too. Most of the animals are dogs and cats. But they've also seen guinea pigs, tortoises, pygmy slow lorises, and tree kangaroos. Clare has even handled animals like flamingos and the rare snow leopard.

Animals have been flying on airplanes through Gatwick Airport for many years. Clare's group works twenty-four hours a day, seven

This turtle was flown to Gatwick Airport on its way to Florida. The airport handles a variety of animals every day.

days a week. They do not just make sure each animal gets where it needs to go. Workers also make sure that every creature is looked after and well fed.

Papers and Passports

Like people, animals need paperwork to travel. There are special papers for animals traveling to or from another country. Pets from European Union countries, such as France and Germany, need a "pet passport." Other countries ask owners to fill out a five-page form. If a pet does not have its proper vaccinations, like a rabies shot, then it must go into quarantine. In quarantine, an animal is held away from other animals. This is to make sure it does not spread illness.

Clare and her team members are one part of a large network at Gatwick Airport. Many people and groups work together to make sure that the airport and air travel run smoothly. The operations, facilities, and workers at all airports play important parts in keeping travelers on the move.

As for the escaped spider, Clare found it. No one, including the spider, was hurt. All in a day's job for Clare.

Chapter 1

FROM GRASSY FIELDS

On December 17, 1903, Wilbur and Orville Wright did something no one had ever done before. The brothers flew a powered airplane in Kitty Hawk, North Carolina.

Today, people use airplanes to travel all over the world. The planes arrive and depart from airports. Sometimes the airports are large buildings with many places for planes to land. Other airports are very small. But none of today's airports look like the place where the Wright brothers flew the first airplane. There were no buildings back then. There were no restaurants, security lines, or roads. Airports have come a long way from the sandy ground at that first flight.

The Wright Brothers and Aerodromes

The Wright brothers' first flight was a big success. But they needed a place to continue their flight testing near their home in Ohio.

Torrence Huffman was a landowner near Dayton, Ohio. He allowed the brothers to use his field outside of town. There, Wilbur and Orville could improve their invention. (They just had to make sure that Huffman's horses and cows did not get loose.) Huffman Prairie Flying Field was a simple, flat field. Wilbur and Orville built three hangars there between 1904 and 1910.

Orville Wright flies his plane while Wilbur watches from the beach at Kitty Hawk, North Carolina.

The Wright brothers traveled across the country to show off their invention. They used golf courses, racetracks, and fairgrounds as their airfields. An airfield is the area of land used for takeoff and landing. There were not any buildings for airplanes or people yet.

Early airports were called aerodromes. Aerodromes were more than simple fields. But they were still easy to use. Takeoffs and landings for planes were done whichever way the wind was blowing. Aerodromes did have better landing fields. They also had some facilities, like places to store equipment. Wilbur Wright set up an aerodrome in College Park, Maryland, in 1909. It is the oldest airfield in the world. There were no buildings for passengers, called terminals, until the 1930s and 1940s.

Sparking Imaginations

In 1908, Wilbur Wright travelled to Paris, France, to show off his new flying machine. People were impressed. One person thought every town would have a port for a flying machine. A port was a town or city with a harbor where ships load or unload their cargo. This person's idea was a port for airplanes instead of ships.

People's imaginations ran wild. Antonio Sant'Elia suggested a giant airplane station in Milan, Italy. Another person, Erich Mendelsohn, imagined a city of the future. He drew plans for an airport made of concrete and steel. A German man named Wenzel

Hablik had an even bolder idea. His dream city floated in the sky among the clouds. It had places to live, work, and land planes.

In the United States, people imagined skyscrapers with launching pads for airplanes. They dreamed of cities with glass buildings, with planes and other machines flying around. But not everyone had such grand ideas. After all, airplanes at the time were still using cow fields as runways.

Post–World War I Construction

After World War I, aerodromes became more popular. People began to see that flying was the future. During the war, the military had set up what would later become airports. London's Beddington Aerodrome was a base from which planes flew to fight German aircraft. Later it became Croydon Airport. Regular people could fly overseas from Croydon. In 1928,

Croydon Airport Firsts

Croydon Airport had many "firsts." It was the United Kingdom's first international airport. It had the first airport hotel in the world. It also had the first customs in the UK. "Customs" means the money people pay when they bring items into or out of a country. Passengers were weighed with their baggage. If they were heavier than a certain weight, they had to pay extra.

Croydon Airport also had the first departure board to help people check their flights. It was really just a wall of clocks that was not too useful. The airport stopped using it after a couple of years.

A mail plane waits to take off from Croydon Airport in 1929.

Croydon opened the world's first air traffic control tower. This was much better than the wooden huts that they had been using!

After the war, Germany was not allowed to spend money on its military. Instead, it put it into aviation—the use of aircraft. Germany's airline, Lufthansa, flew more miles than all European countries combined. The Tempelhof Airport in Berlin was called the best in the world.

Airports Land in America

Americans noticed the airports and air travel in Europe. In 1920s America, air travel was still mostly a private business. The government did not have anything to do with flying. The Air Commerce Act in 1926 changed that. The government became responsible for creating new airways and safety rules. Air travel in the United States began to grow. Cities could now build and run their own airports.

Soon, cities like Buffalo and New York had their own airports. Cleveland, Ohio, set aside 200 acres (80 hectares) for its own airport. Oakland, California, built a terminal, hangars, and the first airport hotel in America. Soon many cities followed their example.

Chapter 2

EARLY AIRPORTS

Charles Lindbergh was an American pilot. He flew nonstop from New York to Paris, France, in 1927. Lindbergh was the first person to fly alone across the Atlantic Ocean. He quickly became a celebrity. Lindbergh toured the United States to promote airports. Airports in the United States improved after Lindbergh's tour.

Clearing for Takeoff

By the mid-1920s, aerodromes, airfields, and aviation fields were all known as airports. An airport was any place where planes, passengers, and cargo could come and go. Many people saw the need for more airports. They tried to get cities to build and operate them. But this was not easy to do.

Many things made it difficult for cities to build and own airports. First, cities needed the government to create new laws. These laws

Charles Lindbergh poses with his plane,
the *Spirit of St. Louis*, in 1927.

would make it legal for them to create a municipal (city-owned) airport. At first, private groups and individuals controlled the airport
projects in their cities. It stayed this way until laws were changed.
Then cities started building municipal airports.

The First "Air Port"

In 1919, Atlantic City, New Jersey, became the first US city to open an "air port." The Atlantic City Air Port was not only an aviation field. It was also supposed to be a mail station and an aerial police station. The city wanted to become a major port city for air and sea transportation. But many of these goals never came to be. The condition of the airfield was poor. Some facilities were incomplete. Others were not built at all. The most lasting effect of the project was the use of the term "air port."

The Military and the Post Office

In the 1920s, the military asked for more airports. It needed a place to train pilots. The military did not have enough money. So it asked private companies to build airports for it. The military printed "how-to" booklets. They explained how to design and build an airport. Tucson, Arizona, was one of the first cities to build an airfield for the military. It was followed by Washington, DC, and others.

Other government groups also wanted more airports. The US Post Office needed more airports to send airmail. It could not afford them. So it worked with cities to build an airmail system. In 1917, Congress gave the Post Office $100,000 for airmail experiments. It found a need for more airports. People from the Post Office traveled the country to get cities to build airports. They decided Atlanta, Georgia, would be a good place for an airport. It took three years to convince the city to build

Lieutenant George Boyle prepares for a flight.
He flew the first mail plane in 1918.

its own airport. It was built on an old racetrack. In 1926, Atlanta finally began receiving airmail. Cities like Chicago soon followed. The Post Office got its airports.

The Post Office became a major player in the airport business. For example, Cleveland, Ohio, had a stop on the airmail route. Rival city Pittsburgh, Pennsylvania, did not want to be left out. That city quickly built its own facilities.

Airports became the "must have" facility of the time. Cities needed an airport if they wanted people to travel there. They also

Passengers wait for their plane in a British airport in 1946. Airports had just started offering more comfortable waiting areas, or lounges.

wanted to keep up with other cities that had one. As more people became interested in flying, more airports were built.

The Lindbergh Boom

After World War I, more people traveled by air. Air traffic increased. This was largely thanks to Charles Lindbergh's flight across the Atlantic Ocean. This time was called the "Lindbergh boom." Lindbergh showed people that air travel was safe.

Interest in flying was so high that the Parker Brothers game company, maker of the board game Monopoly, got involved. It created Aviation: The Air Mail Game in 1929. In the game, two to four players delivered mail to twelve cities across the United States. Players drew cards to choose the destination city and another card for flight conditions.

Comfort Features

Not even the Great Depression could slow down air travel. By 1931, the number of airports had doubled to two thousand. As more people flew, airplanes became larger. Airports had to keep up. New features were built. Runways were paved instead of grass. Terminals gave passengers more than just shelter from the weather. Airports continued to improve. They wanted to show passengers that air travel was safe and modern. The air industry added a national weather service, radio navigation, and air traffic control.

Airports also added commercial features. American Airlines opened the Admirals Club in New York City's LaGuardia Airport in 1939. It was the world's first airport lounge. Airports tried to become a place that people wanted to visit. In 1947, Shannon Airport in Ireland opened the first duty-free shop. People did not have to pay taxes for the items they bought.

Chapter 3

MODERN AIRPORTS

Airports became bigger and more comfortable for passengers. Now people could do a little shopping at the airport. They could also feel good about the safety of air travel. The grassy fields were replaced by pavement runways. New aircraft technology soon changed airports even more.

The Jet Age

The invention of the jet engine was a major event. This new, powerful engine meant planes could fly faster and farther. Frank Whittle from England first tested a jet engine in 1937. Hans von Ohain of Germany was the first to test a jet engine on an aircraft in 1939. The United States soon joined in. It developed the technology during World War II. But it was not widely used until after the war. Newer, larger airplanes such as the 747 came out in the late 1960s. These big airplanes meant airports had to build larger, longer runways.

With faster travel, more people flew. Airports had to grow to make room for all of the travelers. New features, such as a

A US jet goes through testing in 1948. The jet engine allowed planes to fly faster and farther.

The Animal Lounge

At Frankfurt International Airport in Germany, animals are treated well. The Animal Lounge is 40,365 square feet (3,750 square meters). It includes handling and veterinary services. It has housed rhinos from South Africa, hippos from Israel, Chinese lugworms, and many other types of animals.

The airport has twenty-five vets and sixty caretakers for the animals. The lounge makes the animals as comfortable as possible. For example, non-slip asphalt floors are easier on animals' feet than regular concrete. The Frankfurt Animal Lounge is the most modern in the world.

jet bridge, were introduced. A jet bridge is a movable walkway that connects the terminal with the airplane. The new jet planes could travel farther than earlier airplanes. International flight paths changed along with the airports. Airports in smaller cities became less important. Many shut down. Big cities built bigger airports.

Cities began to compete with one another. They all wanted to attract more air travelers. More visitors meant more money. Airports came up with new features. Moving sidewalks helped people get around airports more quickly. New baggage carousels helped passengers get their luggage. Airport terminals were designed to be glamorous. Airports and their terminals were seen as a city's "front door."

Security

Safety became an issue that airports had to address. Starting in the 1950s, airplanes were attacked. Flights in the United States were hijacked. A hijack is when someone forces a pilot to take an airplane where they want to go. Before the 1970s, there was not much security. This changed after airplanes were attacked. Airports started screening passengers and adding airport guards.

Airports started to have more security in the 1970s. Many people did not like the new security checks. They thought airports were taking away their personal rights. But passengers soon saw that the airports were trying to keep them safe.

September 11

Airport security increased after the terrorist attacks on September 11, 2001. On that day, four airplanes were hijacked and crashed, killing thousands. Two planes hit the World Trade Center buildings in New York City. Another plane hit the Pentagon outside Washington, DC. A fourth plane crashed in a field in Pennsylvania. The US government formed the Transportation Security Administration (TSA) to handle security for travelers.

Passengers soon saw a change at the airports. There was more security. Background checks were stricter. Luggage was looked at more closely. New technology was added as well. This included better X-ray machines and body scanners to check for weapons. Airport employees had their criminal backgrounds checked.

Airports Today

Today, airports are designed for comfort and style. New ideas are introduced with each new airport. One example is the Marseille

The terminal at Marseille Provence Airport. In 2013, the airport added thirty new shops and restaurants.

Provence Airport in Marignane, France. Designers made it enjoyable to move through the airport. Passenger areas are very light and modern.

Airports must also be flexible. They have to change when they become more popular. Designers must think of ways to keep lines from getting too long. They might add more security checkpoints. Conveyer belt systems can get luggage through a scanner more quickly.

Designing airports is not done by one person. It is handled by many people with different specialties. The goal is for an airport to be attractive, calming, and easy to get through.

Terminals in Developing Countries

Airports cost a lot of money to build and maintain. Cities and countries expect airports to make money. But sometimes this is not possible. This is especially true in developing countries. These are poorer countries that are trying to improve their economy. For these countries, an airport is mostly about status. It is also a way to bring in tourists, businesspeople, and aid for their people.

Smaller airports are ones that have fewer than one million passengers a year. They rarely offer features like duty-free shops or fine restaurants. They cannot afford these features. But they still offer an important service to their community.

Chapter 4

OPERATION AND RUNWAYS

R unning an airport is complicated. There are many different parts and groups involved. There is much more to it than getting people onto airplanes. Baggage needs to be moved quickly to its proper place. People must be able to find where they need to be to catch their flights. Even the runways have to be placed in a certain way.

Airport Facilities

Runways, taxiways, and aprons are all parts of an airport. They are called the physical facilities. A runway is used for aircraft landing and takeoff. A taxiway is used to move the aircraft around on the ground. The apron is the area where aircraft are parked, loaded, unloaded, refueled, or boarded. Lighting and radio aids make takeoffs and landings safer. Airfields also have special markings, signs, and signals. They help pilots land an airplane and move to the right place on the ground.

Los Angeles International Airport has many terminals, taxiways, and runways.

Airports also have many support facilities. These include weather, fire and rescue, and power. Aircraft and airport maintenance is also a support facility. Terminals, parking, roads, and public transportation are other important parts of the airport. They are called landside facilities.

Airport Management

A lot of work goes on between the terminal and the airplane. This is known as airside services. These services include handling the ramp or jet bridge to get passengers to the aircraft. Other services are baggage and cargo handling, airplane fueling, and airplane cleaning. Checking runways, firefighting, and air traffic control are also part of airside services.

Airports must be ready to help passengers and their baggage get where they need to go. Handling passengers on the ground is called landside services. Check-in, security, customs, and baggage delivery are major parts of landside services. But there are many other ways that airports help passengers. They provide information, catering, cleaning, maintenance, food and beverages, and shops. There is also car rental, special help for the elderly and handicapped, parking, and public transportation.

An airport worker moves baggage onto a plane.

Many different groups help run airports. One group holds the license to operate the airport. That group has overall control. It makes sure the airport runs safely, legally, and smoothly. Other groups handle other airport services. These include the airlines and planes themselves. Air traffic control, ground handling, food stands, and security may all be run by different groups. The government usually runs immigration and customs. It is also responsible for health control and police. Companies provide food for flights, fuel for airplanes, and maintenance. There are also flight clubs and schools that operate out of airports.

Making Money

An airport's main focus is flying. Still, airports make much of their money on the ground. A report from 2017 found that almost half of airports' money came from things not related to aircraft.

Most non-aircraft income comes from parking and ground transportation. Rental cars, stores, and duty-free shopping make up the rest of that income. Airports make money by selling a variety of products, from hair care to technology.

Layout

Airport design is very important. Passengers need to get around an airport easily. A good design makes that possible. Many airports were built decades ago. They must try to improve without building a whole new airport. This is a challenge. People want comfort and options when they travel. For example, major airports all need shopping, leisure, and conference areas.

An airport's layout is the way it is arranged. The layout is often based on the amount of traffic the airport gets. For example, a small airport's layout is usually simple. Smaller airports often have a similar look. As airports become larger, they become more complex. They must meet a unique set of needs. These are different from airport to airport. Unlike smaller airports, layouts of larger airports vary greatly from one another.

Runway Orientation

The orientation of a runway is the direction it faces. Layout and orientation are very important for safety. Runways should not be built near anything that could make flying a plane unsafe. They must avoid obstacles like mountains or buildings.

A crosswind is wind that blows across the direction an aircraft is traveling. In the United States, there are rules about crosswinds. Runways cannot have crosswinds that affect airplanes more than 5 percent of the time. Airports with a single runway must add a second runway if they have too much crosswind.

Different countries have different rules for runways. The runways at Madeira Airport in Portugal run along the coastline. This area has strong crosswinds. It can be a scary place to land or take off!

Sometimes the land where the airport is built limits where a runway can be placed. In these cases, runways may be placed in the shape of the letter V. This gives the airport an option for when the wind is blowing a different direction. For example, Chicago Midway International Airport is built on a small area of land. It must make the most of what is available. It does this by squeezing

Portugal's Cristiano Ronaldo Airport sits next to the Atlantic Ocean. The high winds can make takeoff and landing tricky.

in more runways. The runways are set up so they do not intersect very much. This cuts down on delays since planes don't have to wait for each other.

The small spaces at some airports mean pilots must turn completely around to get back to the terminal. They must be very careful to avoid incoming airplanes. Other airports, such as Dallas/ Fort Worth International Airport have plenty of space. These large airports have enough runways for multiple landings and takeoffs at the same time.

Chapter 5

AIRPORT INDUSTRY

The airport industry continues to grow. There are many jobs that need to be done at airports. One growing area is security. Airport safety has changed a lot in recent years. Many new jobs have been added. Another important area is air traffic control. People who work in air traffic control have a great deal of responsibility. Security and air traffic control are just two career areas for people who want to work in the airport industry.

Security and TSA

The September 11 attacks changed airports around the world. The United States government made major changes to airport security. The Transportation Security Administration (TSA) was formed two months after the attacks. The government hired 65,000 people to be a part of the TSA.

Passengers wait to go through a security
checkpoint at Denver International Airport.

The main goal of the TSA was to make transportation safer. More
passengers needed to be screened. Baggage had to be checked for
bombs or other weapons. The TSA planned on using new technology to help reach its goals.

One of the first jobs of the TSA was to check the background of
750,000 airport employees. It was looking for any criminal activity.
The TSA also added more law enforcement to airports. It made sure
all baggage was screened by X-ray and by hand. It placed more air

Air traffic controllers work in the control tower
at an airport in Montreal, Canada.

marshals on flights. Air marshals are trained to protect passengers
if there is an attack on a flight. The TSA also did more background
checks on passengers. It checked with the FBI and other watch lists
in search of anyone suspicious.

Passengers noticed the changes. They now had to take their
shoes off at security. They had to remove electronic devices for
screening. New scanning technology let TSA workers see more
than ever before. Carry-on luggage was more carefully searched.
Passengers were also limited to the number of bags they could take

onto a plane. Security lines got longer. Also, no one without a ticket could meet or drop off passengers at the terminal gates. The security area was as far as they could go.

Air Traffic Control

In the early days of air travel, airlines handled their own air traffic control. The first Airway Traffic Control Center was built by the airlines in Newark, New Jersey. Centers soon opened in Cleveland and Chicago. Airlines used radio technology to direct where airplanes should go to avoid any issues.

Everything changed in the 1930s. Several deadly accidents happened at that time. One of these was the crash of a DC-2 airplane in 1935. The crash killed New Mexico senator Bronson Cutting. Because of the accident and the senator's death, the US government decided to make some changes. It created a national system of air traffic control. In 1936, the Commerce Department took over air traffic control of flights across the country. By 1938, airport control towers were everywhere.

Today, air traffic controllers use computers and radar to track planes. At busy airports, there can be many air traffic controllers working to track a large number of planes. They must control the airplane traffic on the ground as well as in the air. Air traffic controllers have an important and often stressful job. They are responsible for the safety of many people.

Working at the Airport

Security and air traffic control are two important areas for airport jobs. There are also many other workers who help an airport run smoothly.

Local Flavors

Most of the food at airports comes from well-known brands that can be found everywhere. But some airports are starting to offer more of the area's local food. These airports are adding local restaurants to their terminals. This began in the mid-nineties. At San Francisco International Airport, most of the food is from local brands. A report showed that the airport's food sales went up by more than 50 percent.

National brands have started to compete. Some now offer local flavors on their menus. Auntie Anne's, an American pretzel company, is one example. Its airport stands offer jalapeño pretzels in its Southwest locations.

Skycaps help passengers as soon as they arrive at the airport. They handle luggage and often check in bags right at the curb. They assist disabled passengers. Skycaps also give passengers information and directions. These airport employees usually receive tips.

There are many opportunities for those who want to work directly with aircraft. Workers guide the airplanes as they approach or leave the terminal. Some workers put fuel in the planes. Still others fix and maintain the aircraft. Each job requires special training.

Baggage handlers must make sure that passengers' belongings get where they need to go. They load the baggage onto the plane and remove it when it arrives. They have to be careful to place it in the correct location so it does not get lost.

Another large part of airport work is food service. From food stands to fancy restaurants, lots of people work to give passengers snacks or meals while they wait for a flight.

How Airports Grow

Airports today continue to grow. Domestic flights, or flights within the same country, have increased. But international flights have increased even more. For airports, this means larger planes, more passengers with more baggage, and bigger runways. Airports must grow as the number of passengers grows.

Smaller airports have also grown in number. These airports offer cheaper flights over shorter distances. They attract travelers who normally travel by car, bus, or train. These airports help increase the local tourist economy.

Challenges Ahead

More people are flying than ever before. Still, airports want to attract even more passengers. They are doing this by giving passengers better experiences. This means more training for employees. It can also mean thinking of the airport's place in the community. More airports are starting to consider their effect on the environment.

A food court at an Atlanta airport. Airports
attract many restaurants and businesses.

Airlines and airports work closely together to reach their goals.
They know that they must understand one another and cooperate.
If they do, then they can help each other with getting and keeping
customers. Airlines and airports know that today's passengers want
more from their air travel than before.

Chapter 6

AIRPORTS LOOK TO THE FUTURE

Airports have come a long way from the days of grass runways. They have become key parts of infrastructure. They help people go anywhere in the world. Many of the top airports today are changing what an airport can be.

Top Airports Today

Airports around the world are trying new things with design and technology. In 2007, an airport in Detroit received $5.1 million to cut down on emissions. These are gases that airplanes gives off. They harm the environment and increase pollution. Detroit's new terminal cut emissions by changing how airplanes get their fuel. New fuel hydrants have taken the place of fuel trucks. Fewer trucks means lower emissions.

These solar panels are located at Denver International Airport. The sun's energy provides power for heat and electricity at the airport as well as homes in the area.

In Germany, Düsseldorf International Airport uses green technology. The airport has added 8,400 solar panels. The panels use the sun's energy to provide power. It does not create enough energy for everything the airport needs. But it is the first step toward that goal.

An Australian airport has found a way to help passengers get their baggage quicker. Melbourne International Airport uses a special system to sort up to twenty thousand pieces of luggage each day. The system moves bags through the airport on individual trays. Then it sends each to its proper area by tilting or tipping the bag.

Incheon Airport in Seoul, South Korea, is one of the world's top airports. The airport gives its pilots special technology. It helps with landings when it is difficult to see. Incheon Airport has a large number of travelers with long layovers, or time to wait between flights. The airport gives free services to these travelers. These include a tour of Seoul, showers, and a cultural museum.

Retail

Airport business is going strong. Stores selling electronics, books, and food make money for their owners. In the years to come, they expect to make even more. Some airports think the stores are doing so well because there are more people walking by. More people flying means more people who could buy something. Whenever flights are delayed or missed, more customers shop. Airport spas take advantage of these stressful times. Airport stores are also open more than non-airport stores. Since airports are open on weekends and holidays, the stores are open, too.

Newest Features

Changi Airport in Singapore is one of the best-ranked airports in the world. It is a large, busy airport. But it is not just focused on the passengers. The airport also works to help the environment. The

Gate Service

OTG is a company that lets passengers place orders from airport restaurants and shops using their mobile device. The company then delivers it right to the customer waiting at the gate. Two other companies are starting similar services. Airport Sherpa and At Your Gate deliver anything sold at the airport to anywhere at the airport. For now, the service is only available at certain airports. But keep an eye out! These businesses are growing fast.

airport recycles rainwater instead of letting it run off into a river or ocean. Singapore gets a lot of rainfall in a year. The airport hopes to save water by storing and reusing it.

At Oakland International Airport in California, the TSA is using technology to help with the growing number of passengers. Bins have automated return. Baggage can be checked remotely. Computers can identify explosives in carry-on luggage. This makes the passenger experience easier and safer.

One new airport feature allows people without flights to get to the area beyond security. At Pittsburgh International Airport, people with a special pass are allowed to go to the gate area. Other airports may do the same. The idea is similar to movie theaters that have ticket counters next to the screens. This allows people to come in and buy food and drink without seeing a movie.

Airports of the Future

Today, airports and air travel have come farther than anyone could have dreamed. Airports are no longer just a place to wait for a flight. They are also a place where people can shop, dine, or get a massage.

Technology has played a huge role in changing airports. And even newer technology is on the way. One day we may not need identification cards and boarding passes. Airports are working on

Luxury shops are now common at large airports.

A customs officer uses facial recognition to screen
a passenger at Miami International Airport.

using technology that matches a person's face with his or her passport photo. Fingerprint identification may also be used. Passengers could simply place a finger on a pad before boarding a plane.

Technology will allow people to get where they are going faster, more safely, and more comfortably. The airport industry will continue to change how people view air travel. The airports of tomorrow may look very different from the airports of today.

CHRONOLOGY

1903 The Wright brothers fly the first controlled flight of a powered airplane on December 17.

1915 S. Darius and S. Girėnas, one of Europe's first airports, opens.

1919 The term "air port" is first used in a newspaper article. It refers to Bader Field in Atlantic City, New Jersey.

1926 The Air Commerce Act is passed by Congress. It makes the federal government responsible for starting new airways and setting new rules.

1939 The jet engine is tested on an aircraft on August 27.

1947 Duty-free shops are introduced in Ireland's Shannon Airport.

1973 Airports are required to screen passengers and their carry-on luggage.

1999 Airlines allow their passengers to check into their flights online.

2001 On September 11, terrorists attack the United States using airplanes as weapons. Airport security is raised to new levels.

2001 The Transportation Security Administration (TSA) is created.

2018 JFK Airport in New York City begins testing facial recognition technology to identify passengers as they pass through security.

GLOSSARY

aerial Having to do with aircraft.

aerodrome An area with a landing field for airplanes, buildings, equipment, and shelters.

air marshal An officer who is trained to protect crew and passengers in case of a hijacking.

apron The area outside a terminal where planes load, unload, and refuel.

aviation The operation of aircraft such as airplanes or helicopters.

cargo Goods that are carried on an aircraft.

crosswind Wind blowing across one's direction of travel.

customs Taxes or payments made on things people bring into a country.

domestic Inside a particular country; not foreign or international.

hangar A covered area where planes are kept.

hijack To take control of an airplane by force.

jet bridge A covered, movable connector that extends from an airport terminal gate to an airplane.

layout The way in which the parts of something are arranged.

layover A stop or period of waiting in between two flights on one's trip.

municipal Relating to a city, a town, or its governing body.

orientation The physical position of something.

screen To examine in order to separate from danger.

terminal An airport building where passengers transfer between ground transportation and airplanes.

FURTHER READING

Books

Bordet-Petillon, Sophie, Marc-Étienne Peintre, and Samantha Steele. *The Ultimate Book of Airplanes and Airports.* Paris, France: Twirl, 2017.

Houran, Lori Haskins. *The $25,000 Flight: How Charles Lindbergh Set a Daring Record.* New York, NY: Random House, 2014.

Rhatigan, Joe. *Get a Job at the Airport.* Ann Arbor, MI: Cherry Lake, 2017.

Roby, Cynthia. *Discovering STEM at the Airport.* New York, NY: Powerkids Press, 2015.

Websites

Federal Aviation Administration

www.faa.gov/education/students

Learn about aviation, play games, and more on the Federal Aviation Administration's page for students interested in learning about the aviation industry and careers in the field.

Fun Kids: Amy's Aviation

www.funkidslive.com/learn/amys-aviation

Fun Kids is a children's radio station based in the United Kingdom. Amy's Aviation teaches kids about airplanes, airports, and more.

How Things Fly

howthingsfly.si.edu

The Smithsonian National Air and Space Museum's companion website to its exhibitions offers an interactive way to learn more about flight.

INDEX